Only Through Spiritual Eyes Will You See

Messages

Volume 1

"There is a message in this book for everyone ..."

by ***Avril Hall***

ONLY THROUGH SPIRITUAL EYES WILL YOU SEE

MESSAGES

VOLUME 1

BY AVRIL HALL

FOREWORD BY BISHOP JOHN FRANCIS

Published by Avril Hall
Printed in Great Britain

For more information contact

info@avrilhallglobal.com
www.avrilhallglobal.com

Print ISBN: 978-0-9559944-3-2
EBook ISBN: 978-0-9559944-4-9

Contents

Foreword

Only Through Spiritual Eyes Will You See is a wonderful book that encapsulates powerful scriptures and provides strategies on how to live an abundant life through Jesus Christ, enabling the reader to see their lives through the eyes of the spirit, freeing them from past life experiences and eradicating generational curses.

Throughout the book, the author shares several personal testimonies on how God totally transformed her life and taught her that life's challenges or addictions do not have the final say or determine your future. Avril's relationship with God has certainly had a major impact on her life, and her aim is to encourage the reader that the same will be their testimony, should they accept the Lord Jesus as their Personal Saviour.

The book concludes by asking the question *'Are you ready?'* and prompts the reader to think about their life and the reason why they are here on earth.

Only Through Spiritual Eyes Will You See is a simple and easy read.

Foreword by Bishop John Francis
Ruach City Church, London UK

PREFACE

THIS BOOK IS dedicated to my Lord Jesus Christ who gave me divine insight to write this book. It is also dedicated to all new believers in Christ and to those seeking the Lord Jesus Christ.

Pray and ask the Lord to open your spiritual eyes so that you will see that which I believe the Lord is conveying to His people at this time, a holy nation!

Be blessed!

From a remnant of this last day.

Avril Hall

But the natural man does not receive the things of the Spirit of God, for they are foolishness to him; nor can he know them, because they are spiritually discerned. But he who is spiritual judges all things, yet he himself is rightly judged by no one.

— 1 Corinthians 2:14-15 —

I Cannot Help What I Was Born Into But I Can Change It

I RECALLED HEARING a pastor at my church who was conducting evening Bible Study say, "I don't know what your '*it*' is, but it has to change!" That stayed with me, and I will never forget it. Too often we walk around conducting a pity party, saying things like "Poor me", "Oh, little despised me", "Oh, why me, why did this have to happen to me, to my family ... why, why, why?" Well I have news for you. You can change your life! Why such great faith? I hear you ask. I can say this because I have seen the Lord Jesus Christ change my *it* since I committed my life to Him, over thirteen years ago.

Life is about the choices we make. You can choose life by walking with God (Spirit), or death by walking with the world (flesh). The choices we make in life will determine where we end up. No matter what you were born into, you can change *it*! Think about your *it*. What is your *it*? What is holding you back from reaching your fullness in the Lord Jesus Christ? Is there an area of your life you want to change? Something that has been with you since you had the sense to realise that it should not be so? Does it seem that your family and generations past have had a particular ongoing problem or disorder, and is your family still affected by this *it*? Then firstly, I encourage you to seek Jesus. The Bible says:

> *But seek first the kingdom of God and His righteousness, and all these things shall be added to you* (Matthew 6:33).

"What things shall be added to me?" I hear you ask. Everything you need to change your life, to change your *it* for the better. God gives us the power to change our lives for the good when we accept Him into our lives.

Some people still do not know that the Scripture:

> *Behold, I was brought forth in iniquity, and in sin my mother conceived me* (Psalm 51:5)

applies to us all. They just accept the problem, the disorder, their *it* as something they have to live with - NO! The only life we will know, if we do not know God, is a life of lies. If you do not change your life by accepting the Lord Jesus Christ, that is all you will know, a life of sin and iniquity. The Holy Bible, the word of God says so. Read, meditate and study it, and the truth will be revealed to you.

The Lord can supply all the things you need today, including help with that *it* you want to change:

> *For the word of God is living and powerful, and sharper than any two-edged sword, piercing even to the division of soul and spirit, and of joints and marrow, and is a discerner of the thoughts of the heart.* (Hebrews 4:12).

It is only when you know the truth, which is the word of God, that you can be set free. The greatest truth is that God is the only true God and Jesus Christ is the Son of God. It is by abiding by the word of God that we become a disciple of Jesus Christ:

> *And you shall know the truth, and the truth shall make you free* (John 8:32).

A disciple is someone who is a committed follower of the way of the Lord Jesus Christ and who is adopted into the family of Jesus Christ. By the redemptive blood of Jesus, our sins are washed away and we are then free:

> *Therefore if the Son makes you free, you shall be free indeed* (John 8:36).

You then become a new creature in Christ. When this happens, your way of thinking changes, you do things differently, you no longer go to the places which may cause you to sin, and you no longer associate with those who spoke negativity into your life. All these changes help us to move forward in life:

> *Brethren, I do not count myself to have apprehended; but one thing I do, forgetting those things which are behind and reaching forward to those things which are ahead* (Philippians 3:13).

Move on. Set your mind on the things of Christ. You can receive revelation and insight from God through the Holy Spirit as to why this *it* is hanging around you and your family. By walking with Jesus Christ, meditating on His word, associating with other believers in Christ, and attending a Holy Spirit-filled, Bible-believing church, your situation will turn around. Later on in this book, I explain about paying the price, because everything has a price. With these words of encouragement that I bring into your life, your *it* has to change. But this change comes with a price.

MY TESTIMONY

I was born into a family that did not have much money. Going to school at that time meant walking the three-and-a-half mile journey there and back home, without having any lunch most days because our parents could not afford it. I was born in a country where we appreciated the things around us, the hot weather all year round, lovely sandy beaches, and being able to grow our own food and share it with those less fortunate than ourselves, no matter how we perceived our own situation to be.

I was one of four younger children, and I remember at around fifteen years of age when my mother told us: "Your dad and I do not have any money to send any of you to university when you graduate from high school." I recall a sinking feeling. But then I thought, even though I was not walking with the Lord at that time, my *it* - which was our parents not having the money to send us to university - was not going to stop me doing the best I can attain in life.

At that age, I remember thinking that the world was not going to dictate to me who I should be and that I had a choice in the matter! You see, I knew even then that I cannot help what I was born into, but I can change it! Today, by the grace and mercy of God, and because I seek Him and His kingdom first and all His righteousness, I have been blessed in all areas of my life.

As you read this book, you will begin to see through spiritual eyes what your *it* is, and you too can change your *it*. Develop an attitude of going for gold. Do not allow the situations or circumstances that you see in the natural to dictate to you - you must rise above *it*! Remember, we were all conceived in sin and shaped in iniquity, so ask the Lord Jesus Christ to forgive you of your sins by saying the prayer below:

Dear Lord Jesus,

I believe that You are the Son of God and that You died to save me from my sins. Help me to put You first in my life, Lord, and change my *it* [*name your 'it' here*]. Help me to live a life that is holy and acceptable unto You, Lord. Forgive me of my sins, Lord. Come into my life today, and lead me into the paths of righteousness for Your name's sake.

Amen.

To change your *it*, you must repent and ask the Lord for forgiveness of the sins you have committed, knowingly or unknowingly, past or present. The Lord Jesus wants YOU to come just as you are, no matter where you are at. Do not worry about anything.

May the Spirit of the living God give you the revelation and insight needed to change your *it*! The greatest love of all is the love God shows us:

> *For God so loved the world that He gave His only begotten Son, that whoever believes in Him should not perish but have everlasting life* (John 3:16).

God continues to show His love for His people, and He is ready to come to you right now to help you.

Stop! Thief! How I Robbed God

THE FOLLOWING BIBLE verse used to make me break out in a cold sweat every time I read or thought about it. It reads:

> *"Will a man rob God? Yet you have robbed Me! [God] But you say, 'In what way have we robbed You?' In tithes and offerings* (Malachi 3:8).

When I first became a believer in the Lord Jesus Christ, I did not know anything about tithing. What is tithing? A tithe is one-tenth of what you have, and this is what you give to the Lord.

When my mother took us as children to church, she would put money in an envelope, put her name and details on it and put it in the collection plate as it came through the pews. We used to assist her in preparing it. She did this every month, and she would always give us some coins to put in the collection plate too. We never failed to put something in the collection plate.

When I committed my life to Jesus Christ, I would give what I knew to be an offering, just as I saw my mother do. I would see others in church doing this, so I thought I should do the same; that was all I knew. Then one day, shortly after I gave my life to Christ, my pastor preached on tithing. When he mentioned that we should be giving one-tenth of our earnings to God, everything else he said after that became a blur. Anyone who walks with God and follows Him is called a 'believer in Christ' or a 'Christian', and when you really begin to walk in the ways of the Lord as a Christian, you will experience 'conviction'. Conviction is an instance of feeling convicted about something we realise we should or should not be doing. This is what I experienced as my pastor preached on tithing.

I guess it was the shock of realising that I may have been robbing God without knowing it, and also that I would now have to give to the work of God, money which I had become used to keeping! The Holy Spirit has a way of speaking to our inner spirit when we surrender our lives to God. I realised that I was a thief, and it had to stop.

My head started to spin and all kinds of thoughts came into my mind, like: "I won't have enough money left over to live on," and "I can't give so much money." And so the thoughts went on and on. Then a song came into my head, *"I have decided to follow Jesus, no turning back, no turning back."* Talk about being convicted! I felt like I was being attacked. I thought to myself, it is my money - how dare the pastor preach to me. I was now trying to justify my ways as I did not want to give one-tenth.

The Bible tells us that:

> *Every good gift and every perfect gift is from above and comes down from the Father of lights, with whom there is no variation or shadow of turning* (James 1:17).

God is the one who gives to us freely:

> *And you shall remember the Lord your God, for it is He who gives you power to get wealth, that He may establish His covenant which He swore to your fathers, as it is this day* (Deuteronomy 8:18).

Our God is a covenant-keeping God. A covenant is an agreement between two people or two groups which involves promises made by each to the other. All promises of God, as the word of the Lord says in the Scriptures, will come to pass when we walk according to His will.

> *"So let each one give as he purposes in his heart, not grudgingly or of necessity; for God loves a cheerful giver"* (2 Corinthians 9:7).

Do not bring your gift to God just anyhow. When you give, do so cheerfully! When you come before His presence, always come with an offering. Giving is not just limited to money; it can also mean to give your time, words of encouragement, food, or anything that God has blessed you with.

So from that point onwards I started to tithe, as the word of God clearly says:

> *But be doers of the word, and not hearers only, deceiving yourselves* (James 1:22).

Giving a financial offering in church was no problem for me but I had to learn much on tithing and am still learning. As the Lord directed me in my heart, I would give an offering accordingly. I speak to the Lord about how much He wants me to give, and have covenanted with Him to tithe. The one-tenth of my income was more difficult at first when I received that revelation, but the Lord delivered me, and I do so now cheerfully and without fail. Your tithe must be taken out of your income before you spend on anything else or pay any bills. Do speak to God so that He can bring revelation into your life regarding this area.

After hearing the message on tithing, I knew I had to do the right thing. For years I had robbed God! Yes - I was a thief - it is as simple as that. As the years went on, tithing and giving of offerings became a part of my life, and I started to see things change in my life for the better.

All was going well - or so I thought, until I received another revelation soon after. I was so sure that I was right with God because, of course, I had started tithing and was giving generously to the work of God (towards building His kingdom), and I had started to see blessings manifest in my life. But then one day I switched on the television, and guess what the preacher was talking about - tithing! I got my notebook and pen so that I could take down additional notes on tithing, because I was pleased that all seemed to be going well - after all, I was now a tither. So I listened keenly for further revelation through the message on the television.

You must always be willing to open up and expand your knowledge about the things of God. Have a teachable spirit because there is so much more for you to receive from the Lord.

I then heard the preacher say that tithing should be done based on your gross income and not on the net figure. Now I did not recall hearing my pastor saying this when he had preached on the subject before and wanted to find out from God what I had missed so I started to 'have a word' with God about tithing.

This is how the Lord works. He will send His word as confirmation by any means necessary until we get it right, so be prepared. I could see the words running before my eyes as they started to turn in my head: STOP! THIEF! YOU ARE ROBBING GOD STILL! "Oh, Lord," I thought. "Do you have to give me such revelations that I could really do without?" Once you say yes to the Lord and begin to receive His word, you have no choice but to act on it. That is why you have to come to Him as you are. He is the one who can change you; you cannot change your *it* on your own.

Be *doers of the word, and not hearers only.* (James 1:22).

This is a Scripture I would hear constantly and one which the Lord Jesus keeps on bringing back to my remembrance.

I started tithing on my gross income. God sent His word, and He always will when we have an earnest heart and want to live according to His word. I am seeing God's promises coming through for me, and I know it is because I take heed to His every word. I started to receive financial breakthroughs in the form of job promotions, and also received divine revelation and insight into good money management. When you obey the Lord and live according to His word, breakthroughs will come, blessings will manifest in your life, and this will be a regular occurrence when you continuously walk according to His word.

This is why you should check the things you are doing if things are not going well in your life. Are they 'of' and 'unto' the Lord or have you given the enemy access through your thoughts and actions? Walking in obedience to the word of God is key. This is the price we must to pay to walk holy and acceptable unto the Lord. We must do all that the word of God says and not just some of it! Study and meditate on the word of God daily, and you will receive divine revelation.

When Jesus died for our sins, He rose again on the third day and ascended into heaven to be at the right-hand of God, and He is there right now interceding on the believers' behalf. When Jesus left this earth to be with the Father, He said:

> *And I will pray the Father, and He will give you another Helper, that He may abide with you forever* (John 14:16).

Jesus continued:

> *But when the Helper comes, whom I shall send to you from the Father, the Spirit of truth who proceeds from the Father, He will testify of Me* (John 15:26).

God will never leave us nor forsake us. He will always send help to His people. Through the Holy

Spirit's help and guidance, we are made aware of what God requires of us as believers in Christ. It is important to be in fellowship with other believers in Christ, those who are living by the word of God. Find a Bible-believing, Holy Spirit-filled church to attend, and attend regularly so you can grow spiritually.

I use every opportunity to tell others about good money management, tithing, giving an offering and giving of their time and other resources to assist others, thereby building the Kingdom of God. We cannot give to building the kingdom of God or others without first having love in our hearts, love for God and love for one another.

Lord, When You Are Sending Someone To Me, Send Gabriel!

THERE ARE ANGELIC beings that work on behalf of every believer in Christ. Angels are messengers from God. The angel Gabriel was symbolic of a 'type' of Christ. Sometimes we settle for second best and we do not go for gold! As I mentioned in the first chapter of this book, whatever we are born into - which is sometimes not the way of the Lord - without revelation from the Holy Spirit, we will often see the same thing move from generation to generation. I encourage you to confess your sins, repent, and ask God to release angelic beings to work on your behalf. If you are walking fully as the Lord Jesus requires of you, then as Scripture highlights:

> *"And whatever things you ask in prayer, believing, you will receive"* (Matthew 21:22).

Walk in the ways of the Lord, and ask God for the best He has for you. There are many people in the Bible who had angelic encounters. Mary was told by the angel Gabriel of the virgin conception and birth of Jesus (Luke 1:26-38). Zechariah was visited by angel Gabriel regarding John the Baptist (Luke 1:13-19), and Manoah's family was visited by an angel several times and given the promise of Samson's birth (Judges 13:2-21). When an angel of the Lord appears, great things happen in the lives of those who encounter this divine visitation.

Satan was once an angel of God. His name then was Lucifer, which means "fallen one". When he was thrown out of heaven, his name became Satan, also known as the devil, the enemy. Satan imitates the things of God, and that is why when you do not know God or what the word of God says, you are in bondage to the things of Satan. If you walk in accordance with the Spirit of God, then you are no longer a slave to sin. This means that you are no longer in bondage but free:

> *Therefore you are no longer a slave but a son, and if a son, then an heir of God through Christ* (Galatians 4:7).

God is our Father and, like any parent, He wants the best for His child. Nothing that comes from God is mediocre, it is all good. Anything that brings sorrow with it is not of God, so strive to get the best that God has for you. Surround yourself with people who speak positivity into your life, and stay away from those who always have negative things to impart. Pray and ask God to send those ordained by Him into your life. Just as God will send people into your life to take you to the destination He has ordained for you, Satan will also send people into your life to pull you away from the things of God and to lead you down the road of destruction. Walk in discernment. Discernment in this context, is the ability to tell the difference between that which is of God and that which is not. Pray for Godly wisdom:

> *Wisdom is the principal thing; Therefore get wisdom. And in all your getting, get understanding* (Proverbs 4:7).

> *But solid food belongs to those who are of full age, that is, those who by reason of use have their senses exercised to discern both good and evil* (Hebrews 5:14).

If it looks good, sounds good, but does not bear the fruit of the Spirit, then it is not of God. God will remove people from your life who try to stop His purpose and plan for your life. He may just remove them for a season as you develop and mature in the things of God, or it may be forever. The main thing is that you should put your trust in the Lord your God. This is why the walk with God can be a very lonely one because you need to:

> *Enter by the narrow gate; for wide is the gate and broad is the way that leads to destruction, and there are many who go in by it. Because narrow is the gate and difficult is the way which leads to life, and there are few who find it* (Matthew 7:13-14).

It can be a lonely walk, because you may not find many people on the same level as you in Christ. Not many people are prepared to make the sacrifices necessary to follow wholly after God. Some people often say to me that my conversations are "deep", and then they will withdraw from me; this is because we are not at the same level in Christ. When you study the word of God, your speech, actions, outlook on life and everything else changes for the better - and you may find that many do not share the same level of commitment and determination as you, just keep going.

Deciding to follow Jesus means giving up the things of the flesh, our *it*, and the things of the world - fleshly things:

> *Now the works of the flesh are evident, which are: adultery, fornication, uncleanness, lewdness, idolatry, sorcery, hatred, contentions, jealousies, outbursts of wrath, selfish ambitions, dissensions, heresies, envy, murders, drunkenness, revelries, and the like of which I tell you beforehand, just as I told you in time past, that those who practice such things will not inherit the kingdom of God.* (Galatians 5:19-21).

Remember we were all brought forth in iniquity, and our mothers conceived us in sin (Psalm 51:5). We must, therefore, turn away from fleshly things and turn to the things of God, which are of the Spirit. We must bear good fruit.

> *But the fruit of the Spirit is love, joy, peace, long-suffering, kindness, goodness, faithfulness, gentleness, and self-control. Against such there is no law* (Galatians 5:22-23).

You cannot live of the flesh and of the Spirit. You must choose! Remember, life is about the choices we make, and living in eternity is about making the right choice. The 'natural man' is a person who does not walk according to - and therefore cannot understand - the things of God.

> *But the natural man does not receive the things of the Spirit of God, for they are foolishness to him; nor can he know them, because they are spiritually discerned. But he who is spiritual judges all things, yet he himself is rightly judged by no one*
> (1 Corinthians 2:14-15).

To walk in discernment you must have a relationship with God. God is a God of relationship - it is not about what we do – but how sincere we are when we are doing it. You cannot say you know God and that you are walking in His ways, and then the next moment you are walking with the devil (Satan) and doing things which do not bear good fruit. The Lord will release to us just what we need, when we need it.

Today, if you know and believe in the Lord Jesus Christ, ask Him to release to you the best He has for you! As you are now reading this book, you can no longer say that you are ignorant of the word of God. You must choose today whom you will serve. You cannot serve God and the devil. *'If God be God, serve Him'*.

It Is a Sect. Tear Away From It!

As I OUTLINED in the first chapter, although you were born into a particular lifestyle, it does not mean you have to remain in it!

Jesus spoke of hypocrites who fast:

> *"Moreover, when you fast, do not be like the hypocrites, with a sad countenance. For they disfigure their faces that they may appear to men to be fasting. Assuredly, I say to you, they have their reward"* (Matthew 6:16).

When you confess and repent of your sins, ask the Lord for forgiveness and turn away from your sinful ways. You have to walk according to the Spirit of God. Whatever we do as believers in the Lord Jesus Christ, we must do as unto the Lord. The Lord is not looking for 'show-offs' - He is not moved by this - He made us! The Lord is looking for those who have a heart after Him, those who will build His kingdom and not build up riches for themselves.

Every believer in Jesus Christ must stay focussed on the word of God, and constantly check themselves to ensure that they are not caught up in religious acts. God is not interested in religious acts.

> *But the hour is coming, and now is, when the true worshippers will worship the Father in spirit and truth; for the Father is seeking such to worship Him."* (John 4:23)

Worship God for who He is and not for what you can get from Him!

> *But seek first the kingdom of God and His righteousness, and all these things shall be added to you* (Matthew 6:33).

My Testimony

When my mother would take us as children to church, I used to find it a real chore. Sometimes she would drag my father along. I would utter, "Oh no, not church again!" I used to think back then that going to church was boring and a waste of time, and I stopped going the first chance I got when I came of age.

I now know that it was the devil's strategy to try to keep me out of the will of God. I did not understand what all the fuss was about back then, and I used to think church people were crazy! These are all lies from the pit of hell, from the devil (Satan) and his entourage! There is another side to all this when you come to know the Lord Jesus and His word, which is the truth. You move from the lies of Satan, to the truth which is God.

Some people go so far as to get caught up in religion or religious acts. Some people attend church because their parents attended church, and maybe they were forced to go. This is an example of how one can get caught up in religious acts from generation to generation, because it was what they were born into. It is what they knew their parents or others before them did. It is when the Spirit of God draws you to Himself and you receive a revelation for yourself and act upon the word of God, that you see things happen in your life; you begin to realise that you are not merely following what you saw folks before you do, but you are doing what God requires of you.

However, some people will go to church every Sunday but never get the revelatory word of God. Why? Because it is like a sect to them. Some attend because they like the preacher or are seeking welfare. News flash: time is short; Jesus is coming back soon! We all need to look at why we do certain things.

What is the motive behind what we do? Is it to build the Kingdom of God and to give Him all the glory or is it for selfish gain? What spirit is behind what we do? Who are we aiming to please? Is it to serve and please God by winning souls for His kingdom? Is it to get closer to Him - to have His character, His mind, His heart? Is it to bless others as the Lord blesses us or is it for us to keep to ourselves? If your answers to these questions show that your motives are for selfish gain, ask the Lord Jesus to show you how to move on. He is willing and ready to assist you.

All that you do must be as unto the Lord, and only to Him. Apply what the word of God says to your life so that you are in right standing with God:

But be doers of the word, and not hearers only deceiving yourselves (James 1:22).

Do not hold on to the things of the world just because it seems easier and less questionable. Satan has a field day with his workers of iniquity because they are in the dark! If a person has not given their life over to Christ, then they are in darkness, for God is light. As children of the Most High God, we must tear away from certain things in our lives that hold us in bondage to the world. These are called 'strongholds'. Compromise is not an option in the Kingdom of God. If you are to walk holy and acceptable in God's sight, you must tear away from bad habits, and from the things that keep you from walking fully in what God has promised in His word to do for you. In the Kingdom of God there is no fence to sit on. You are either for Him or against Him. There are no two ways about it. (Study the Book of Revelation, chapters 1-3).

Once you commit your life to the Lord, the Holy Spirit will work in you and bring you to a place where you feel uneasy if you are not doing what God requires of you. This is called 'being convicted', which I talked about in the second chapter. If you still commit sin and feel no way about it, then you are not walking with God. You must give the Lord Jesus your all. Feed on His word, do His will, and abide by and be a 'doer' of the word of God.

You will know if the things you do are of God when the word of God bears witness with your spirit. Ask the Lord to tear you away from things that will harm you and which are leading you down the road of self-destruction. How do you know what these are? They are things which do not line up with the word of God. Read, meditate and study the word of God and fellowship with other believers in Christ. If your life does not bear any resemblance to the word of God, then it is a sect, tear away from it!

If You Did Not Pay The Price For It, You Cannot Have It!

> *For the wages of sin is death, but the gift of God is eternal life in Christ Jesus our Lord* (Romans 6:23).

TO LIVE ETERNAL life, you must choose life. As I have mentioned before, life is about choices. The Lord not only gives us a choice in His word, but He also gives us the right choice. With that, the right thing to do is clear. The Bible tells us:

> *Enter by the narrow gate; for wide is the gate and broad is the way that leads to destruction and there are many who go in by it,* because narrow *is the gate and difficult is the way which leads to life and there are few who finds it* (Matthew 7:13-14).

Nothing in this life is free, EVERYTHING has a price. Life has a price and death has a price. Life is truth and death is all lies:

> *But now having been set free from sin, and having become slaves of God, you have your fruit to holiness, and the end, everlasting life* (Romans 6:22).

Therefore, if you are not free, you are in bondage and heading for death. You cannot live as the world lives and say you have Christ in you. Some people think that in order to come to Christ, they must be perfect, but Jesus works with us just as we are; no one is perfect. Jesus is the potter and we are the clay, He moulds us into what we should become.

When I first gave my life to Christ after He drew me unto Himself, I wondered how I would let go of the things I was 'enjoying' in the world. You see, you are born into the world, so that is the only life you will know, a life of bondage. When the truth - which is the word of God - is established in your life, you are set free. The things of the world are nothing compared to the joy you have in Christ

Jesus! Just ask anyone who walks closely with God; they have peace.

> *And the peace of God, which surpasses all understanding, will guard your hearts and mind through Christ Jesus* (Philippians 4:7).

For some people, leaving the things of the world behind is an area that they still struggle with, and it will be particularly difficult it they do not fully let go and allow God into their hearts. Some people will still want to hold onto the things of the world because that was all they knew. Even as a new believer in Christ, you can slip into bad habits because you do not yet know fully the word of the Lord. Repent and ask God for forgiveness, and if you genuinely mean it from your heart, you will get back on track. Pray and ask God for wisdom. The more you follow after God, read, study and meditate on His word, the more you will want nothing to do with the things of the world. It was only when I started to go deeper into the word of God that sin no longer had dominion in my life. God's grace is sufficient for you; it will see you through all that life throws at you:

> *For sin shall not have dominion over you, for you are not under law but under grace* (Romans 6:14).

Everything has a price. If you decide to walk fully with God, there is a price to pay! The price is to live a life that is holy and acceptable unto the Lord. What I have now, knowing that Jesus paid the ultimate price for me by dying on the cross for my sins and rising again after the third day - is better than anything that Satan could ever give me for free! Even then, what Satan gives (a life of sin), is not even free for the Bible tells us:

> *"The wages of sin is death, but the gift of God is eternal life in Christ Jesus our Lord."* (Romans 6:23)

Sin has a price, and you have to pay; it is death, and the gift of God has a price, it is eternal life, it pays to walk wholly after God!

There are no regrets in my life since I gave my life to Christ when He drew me unto Himself. Jesus was hung on a cross just for you and for me; He paid the ultimate price. All you have to do now is say, "Yes, Lord, I will follow wholly after You."

Some people are not prepared to pay the price for eternal life because they want something for nothing. They want a life that seems to match up with the world's standards, where they are not accountable to anyone and can do as they wish. This is where Satan entices them. It looks like it is free, but it is not, because everything has a price. Satan is a counterfeit, a liar and a deceiver. He makes things look, feel and taste good to the natural senses, but it is all lies; it is deception! Satan comes to steal, kill and destroy God's plan for our lives. If you are walking with God, then the Bible declares:

> *"So shall they fear the name of the Lord from the west, and His glory from the rising of the sun; when the enemy comes in, like a flood the Spirit of the Lord will lift up a standard against him"* (Isaiah 59:19).

Jesus unwraps the package of His promises to you in His word. You must meditate on the word of God, know the word of God and declare the word of God out loud. The enemy would wish for believers in Christ to keep quiet, but you must shout! Just as Jesus made a great sacrifice for us all, you will have to make sacrifices to live a life that is holy and acceptable unto God. Things you used to do that is not of God, has to stop.

The renewing of your mind is essential. You will need to put off the 'old man' and take on the 'new man', as the Bible tells us in Colossians 3:9-10, which is a process. It starts by confessing that Jesus Christ is the Son of God, and that you believe Jesus died for your sins and rose again. Ask God to show you areas in your life (your *it*) that do not line up with His word, and He will change you.

> *Ask and it will be given to you, seek and you will find; knock and it will be opened to you* (Matthew 7:7).

The Lord will do wonderful works in your life and bring His goal to completion. The word of God does not lie:

> *God is not a man, that He should lie, nor a son of man, that He should repent. Has He said, and will He not do? Or has He spoken, and will He not make it good?*
> (Numbers 23:19).

There is a race to run, and the finishing line requires believers in Christ not only to finish, but to finish well. Remember, if you did not pay the price for it, you cannot have it.

Rhema, Can I Have a Word?

EVERY DAY I listen with my spiritual ear to hear a word from the Lord for my personal circumstances. Some of the ways I receive the word of God include reading the Bible, meditating on the word of God, praying to God, fellowshipping with other believers in Christ and by going to church. In doing so, an answer will usually come through in one of several ways, either through the leading of the Spirit of God to a Scripture verse or through various other situations or circumstances.

God also speaks through people or inanimate objects; He has spoken to me through bill boards! The Lord will send His word for you through whatever means you will be attentive. At times, He will even use unbelievers to deliver His word! Ask God today for a word specifically for you, for whatever it is you are facing. This is what a 'rhema' word is: a word inspired by God within your spirit just for you.

God sends His word to assist us. Jesus is risen. He is alive, He died for us and rose again after the third day, so He is not like the gods that other people worship - He is alive and hears His children when they call. Just as many instruction manuals exist, there is also an instruction manual for everyone who wants to live eternal life called The Holy Bible, the living word of the Most High God:

> *For prophecy never came by the will of man, but holy men of God spoke as they were moved by the Holy Spirit* (2 Peter 1:21).

The Bible was written by chosen prophets of God as the Spirit of God moved within them. The Bible is known as the 'logos' - the written word of God which is for everyone.

Jesus is the 'King of kings' and 'Lord of lords' and there is no other God besides Him! If you are not worshipping God, Jesus Christ, and the Holy Spirit (for the three are One), then you are worshipping an idol. Idolatry is anything that takes the place of a 'god' in your life that you worship. Jesus Christ is the one true and living God. People can worship their home, job, clothes, car, other people, a carved object, or anything that is the centre of their focus other than God.

If you are worshipping anyone or anything other than God, pray to God right now, confess it, repent and turn to the Lord Jesus. Ask God to show you anything in your life that you are worshipping apart from Him, and ask Him to get rid of it from your life.

> "*And again I say, it is easier for a camel to go through the eye of a needle than for a rich man to enter the kingdom of God*". (Matthew 19:24)

Pray to God for a rhema word so that you can draw closer to Him and serve and worship Him alone.

I am a testimony of what the Lord can do. He changed me from being a rebellious, unruly person to being His friend and someone who has a love for others. If God can do it for me, He will do it for you. Just obey and trust in Him. Commune with Him in prayer and in daily devotion. Feed on His every word; it is spiritual food, and God will reveal a rhema word to you for your personal situation.

Are you receiving a word from Him directly or are you allowing people to speak into your life? The title of this book is, '*Only Through Spiritual Eyes Will You See - Messages*', and I sense that the Lord gave me this title because the things that He has led me to write will not be understood by the natural man, nor those who are not walking in accordance with the will of God. They will not be able to understand what the Lord has divinely led me to write in this book. He is specifically preparing His people for the end times, and there is a remnant that is on fire for God; people who are hungry for a word and committed to walking with Him no matter what.

In each chapter of this book, the Lord has, I believe, divinely and strategically given a word for everyone who reads it! There is a word for everyone - you just have to search it out. As you read, have your Bible and note paper to hand. Do your own study, and allow the Holy Spirit to lead and guide you:

> *It is the glory of God to conceal a matter, but the glory of kings is to search out a matter* (Proverbs 25:2).

Search the Scriptures for a word from God. Pray and devote time daily to being in His presence and seeking His face. You are nourished if you constantly feed on something good, and the things of God are good. Do not allow yourself to become spiritually malnourished by only occasionally spending time with God or rarely reading or studying His word.

When you have the word of God inside you, it becomes easily accessible when challenges come into your life. The word of God will be there straight away to bring peace, comfort, joy and strength. The word will also be there ready to encourage someone else, to build them up and to bring peace and comfort into their lives too. When you know the word of God, the way you deal with challenges, or with someone who needs a helping hand, will be different compared to someone who does not know the word of God.

Rather than leaving it to the preacher to receive a word from the Lord on your behalf, search out the word of God daily for yourself. The word of the Lord is truth; it brings life. Some people will only go to church to hear a word from the preacher, wondering if God told the preacher anything to prophesy about their situation, and this is all they depend on. If they feel that they did not get a word from God through the preacher, they start to become disappointed with God or with the preacher, and may even move away from God's will for their lives. Read the word of God for yourself so you can get a revelation for yourself; you will then know that your relationship with God is developing as you depend only on Him. Do not just depend on going to hear the preacher or on what someone else may write or speak into your life. Remember this of the Lord:

> *"Your word is a lamp to my feet and a light to my path"* (Psalm 119:105).

Develop a relationship with God. Some of the ways that you can do this include spending time every day in His presence, praying and reading His word. The Lord is a gentle God and a faithful God. He will never leave us nor forsake us, and neither does He force Himself on us.

"Behold, I stand at the door and knock. If anyone hears My voice and opens the door, I will come in to him and dine with him, and he with Me
(Revelation 3:20).

Even when we are not faithful, God remains faithful and will never turn His back on His chosen ones - those who believe and trust in Him. Make time for Him each day, and keep your spiritual sword sharp! We are living in the last days, the end times, a time when Jesus is returning to take those who have been living righteously back with Him (the remnant). Jesus reminds us of this:

> *"In My Father's house are many mansions; if it were not so, I would have told you. I go to prepare a place for you"* (John 14:2).

There is coming a time when those who are righteous, who live by His word and do the will of God, will be with Him.

> *The steps of a good man are ordered by the Lord; and He delights in his way*
> (Psalm 37:23).

We all stumble from time to time, but when we repent and stay in the word of God, we will get back up again. The Lord does not hold those who truly love Him in condemnation when they repent and turn from their sinful ways. Develop a spirit of repentance so that you remain on track:

> *There is therefore now no condemnation to those who are in Christ Jesus, who do not walk according to the flesh, but according to the Spirit* (Romans 8:1).

You need to know the word of God so that you can follow Him, know how to conduct yourself, and know how to deal with any circumstances or situations that may arise. Apply the word! When you know the word, Jesus is right there with you because He is the Word. The word is truth and brings life. God knows our situation because He is omnipotent and omniscient, He is everywhere and knows everything at the same time. Take everything to Him in prayer, and He will give you a word for your situation.

When you ask God for a word, you need to have your spiritual ears open to hear what the Spirit of God is saying. He will bring you peace:

> *Be still, and know that I am God; I will be exalted among the nations, I will be exalted in the earth!* (Psalm 46:10).

The word of God steers us in the right direction and steers us away from unrighteous paths. God must get all the glory. He must be exalted throughout this earth.

What does the word of God say about your situation or circumstance? Ask yourself, "Now what would Jesus do?" This should be the question on your lips before making any decision or moving in any direction. This is why you must be aware of false prophets. They come with smooth words, and if you do not know the truth, which is what the word of God says - you can be deceived. Have faith in God alone, not faith in man. What is Godly faith?

> *Now faith is the substance of things hoped for, the evidence of things not seen* (Hebrews 11:1).

This is why new creatures in Christ are called Christians or believers in Christ, because they need to believe in things that are not seen. They walk by faith and not by sight. Our walk with God is based upon believing in Christ Jesus. How then can I have faith in God? Scripture tells us how:

> *So then faith comes by hearing, and hearing by the word of God* (Romans 10:17).

The word of God did not say that faith comes by "hearing any word", it says that faith comes by hearing "the word of God"; there is a difference.

You were led to this book for a reason, and the reason is that you need a word from the Lord!

Cursed, Who? That Is Past Generations

As a believer in the Lord Jesus Christ, you should not be under any generational curses. Curses are the reverse of blessings which can be passed down from generation to generation, or through a door you have opened that is not of God, or because someone may have spoken it over your life. Believers in Christ are armed by the word of God, and because of this, they know how to break chains and bondage from past sinful iniquities. Some people today have opened doors in their lives which allow Satan - the enemy, and the whole host of darkness to enter, and are thereby living a cursed life.

Are things in your life working differently to what God has said in His word for your life? Check to see if you are doing anything contrary to the word of God. If so, bring it to the Lord in prayer, confess it, repent and turn away from it - and shut the door! If you are truly sorry, the Lord is waiting to forgive you, no matter what you have done. Generational curses can be broken in the name of Jesus. Identify *it*, plead the blood of Jesus against it, then say this prayer from your heart:

Dear Lord Jesus,

I believe You want to bless me. I therefore renounce all sins of past generations that have been passed down to me or my family through my bloodline or through spoken words or ungodly covenants or soul ties.

I ask you, God, through the blood of Jesus Christ which was shed for me, that all curses, whether passed down through past generations or which I have knowingly or unknowingly brought upon myself or my family, be removed today. I repent for the curse(s) of [*name the curse(s) here if you know what they are*], and I ask You, Lord Jesus, for forgiveness and believe You have set me and my family free.

I thank You, Lord Jesus, for forgiveness of these sins, I now walk in Your blessings as ordained for my life and my family's life, now and for generations to come.

I thank You that the blood of Jesus Christ covers me, my family, my child(ren), their children and generations to come, and I ask for Your protection from the plans and devices of the enemy.

In Jesus' name,

Amen.

MY TESTIMONY

When I first came to live in England, my first permanent job was at the headquarters of a wine merchant. First thing each morning, staff would be given the choice to taste newly released wines and to take home any unfinished bottles at the end of the day. It was natural, I thought, to be in this environment because I grew up around alcohol.

When I was growing up, my mother - who has always been a firm believer in Jesus Christ and walks according to the word of God - did not drink alcohol, but it was not so with my father. At times on our way home from school, my youngest brother and I would meet him in public houses where everyone also drank alcohol, some to the point of intoxication. At home on special occasions, I recall that my father would prepare a cocktail of drinks when visitors came to our home, and he would let me have 'a taste'.

My youngest brother and I in particular, seemed to have developed a taste for strong drink when we became adults. Having a taste for alcohol was 'normal' for me, and working in a wine merchant was then nothing to me. This was also my first permanent job, so how could I not take it! Alcohol, I later realised, was my *it*, a curse and a stronghold in my life.

Drinking a whole bottle of wine with meals or whilst watching television and socialising was normal for me before I surrendered to God. After a while I became uncomfortable working at the wine merchants for some unknown reason; I know now that it was the Lord pulling me away, or it would have messed up my life. I resigned soon after that as the job became extremely burdensome, I was restless, lacked focus and was tired all the time.

Leaving work under the influence of alcohol and still having to pick up my baby daughter from the child-minders at the time was a wake-up call. The sound of rattling bottles of alcohol in my bag leftover from the day's wine tasting session at work became scary. I thought then that I was turning into an alcoholic! This was a sobering thought. I had not received my deliverance at that point because I was still operating in the flesh. I just could not break free, no matter how I tried. Although I knew deep down that I needed to stop drinking, I could not. I would try not to buy alcohol but soon started again as my flesh craved for it, I was weak. The people I associated with then, also drank, and I would end up going to parties and drinking until I was intoxicated, but I felt that I could handle it. This was all lies from the enemy - I know that now.

Although I was cautious about drinking and driving, I slipped up one night. I had gone to a friend's birthday party, and she invited me to have just one small glass of wine. Although I said "no" initially, she persuaded me, and I had a drink or maybe two or more. I cannot recall my journey home, but I remembered leaving her house, she did not live far from me, getting into my car and then arriving home. The battle with alcohol went on for a while.

Then one New Year's Eve night, just over thirteen years ago, I was invited to another friend's party, where I had too much to drink. Although I was intoxicated, I had a sobering moment! I recall speaking to the Lord. I told Him that this life was not for me: drinking alcohol just like my father used to do (that generational thing) and not heading in the direction that I needed to go in. For years I had felt an emptiness deep inside and, at the time of this encounter, I had long since stopped attending church and reading the word of God. I knew I was searching for something as there was a void, but I did not know or understood what this void was.

Having a belief that you can handle something that is not good for you (operating in the flesh) keeps you in bondage and slowly destroys you. If your flesh is stronger than your spirit man, then it will rule you and take you down unrighteous paths which you may think you can handle, but it is a lie from hell. It is Satan's destructive plan for your life.

Although I was not saved, my mother always ensured that we lived a Godly life, so I constantly had 'words' with God. That New Year's Eve night, I recall giving God an ultimatum. Yes, me as an unbeliever back then giving God an ultimatum! I told the Lord that He had "better find me a decent church to attend", and that this was "my last night of drinking alcohol" because I was tired of it. You see, the Lord knows each and every one of us. When we are in sin, our eyes are spiritually blinded. But God made us, so He will always come and rescue us when we call on Him and want to live righteous.

You may ask, "If God knows, why does He not just do it anyway?" When God created the earth, He then created man to have dominion over the earth, to be fruitful and multiply (Study Genesis 1 to 3). God does things in order, and God’s order is that we must come to Him. I did not know the plans

God had for my life. I did not know that I would be writing this book for others to read, sharing what the Lord has done for me, sharing my testimonies and showing what the Lord can do for them too. My life has not been the same, and now I am on fire for God.

Shortly after my encounter that night the Lord led me to a Bible-believing, Holy Ghost-filled church. Within seven months, one day during a church service, I surrendered my life to the Lord Jesus Christ. Now as a believer of the Lord Jesus Christ, He has shown me that what I went through with alcohol was a stronghold, that alcohol was my *it*. Through surrendering to the Lord Jesus Christ, I have been delivered from alcohol. I know that God's will and purpose for my life must be fulfilled and that Satan will try to use anything he can to try and stop it.

> *"Yet in all these things we are more than conquerors through Him who loved us."* (Romans 8:37)

It is only through taking your *it* to the Lord in prayer that He is able to come through for you.

Your experience will be your weapon. You will use what you have learnt from your experiences in life to move forward in Christ. I have testimonies because I have been through various experiences. Whatever you go through now, you must learn from those experiences, and you too will have testimonies that will help others.

Do take some time to think about the things that are strongholds in your life or your family's lives. What patterns do you see emerging from generation to generation? Look and you will see! *Only through spiritual eyes will you see.* Ask the Lord to reveal strongholds to you so that you will know how to pray strategically to destroy their roots. The Lord will help you.

An uncle and a brother of mine both died from alcoholism, and I have seen other family members afflicted by this. But in the name of Jesus, this is where it stops! It will not move on to any other generation; it is terminated from the roots, in Jesus' name! Alcoholism is a disease, but at the time I could not see that alcohol was a stronghold in my family because I was living in sin. I had not surrendered my life to God and thought what I was doing was normal. Sin blinds our eyes to the truth. The truth is alcohol destroys lives. Alcohol temporarily gives pleasure to the flesh, but it is only when you walk in the Spirit of God that you will be able to see as God sees - through spiritual eyes; then you can ask God to do something about your *it*. You cannot change your *it* on your own, as walking in the flesh keeps you in bondage. This is why you must constantly surrender to God, not just once after you give your life to God, but daily. Surrendering totally and walking according to the Spirit of God will change your *it*.

Curses must be destroyed from the root so that they can be completely removed. You may be the one called by the Lord to stop generational curses from moving down your family line. Be obedient to the leading of the Holy Spirit. The Lord will reveal something to you, and you will receive that revelation either through speaking to a family member, or by studying the word of God. You may have noticed an ongoing pattern of behaviour that is contrary to what God says in His word, or you may see things happening in your family which are destructive - this could be a curse. Read and study Deuteronomy 28 to see what the Bible says about blessings and curses. If a curse is revealed to you, then you are most likely the one who is called by

God to stop it from moving down the family line in the name of the Lord Jesus Christ!

Revelation of this comes when you have a relationship with God. Take it to the Lord in prayer. Ask God to show you how to pray to eradicate this destructive *it* that is in your family:

> *However, this kind does not go out except by prayer and fasting* (Matthew 17:21).

The Lord will reveal to you whether you need to go into a time of warfare prayer, or He may lead you to pray and fast.

You may find that curses are time-bound. You may notice that as a family member reaches a certain age, for instance, something significant happens. They may start to display symptoms of a certain illness, a crave for alcohol and other drugs, sudden or unexplained death, or even on-going disagreement among certain family members as each new sibling. This does not have to be so; it can be eradicated. As curses move from generation to generation, the stronghold becomes greater because the ultimate aim of Satan, the ruler of darkness, is to steal, kill and destroy. He wants people to live in hell! But my God is a good God:

> *Every good gift and every perfect gift is from above, and comes down from the Father of lights, with whom there is no variation or shadow of turning* (James 1:17).

If we give the enemy cause to come in through an open door, repent today and turn from any sinful ways, and see God come through for you and your family.

Prodigal ... Who Me?

ONE THING I am grateful for in my life since the Lord chose me, is that I strive to be righteous in His sight, not in the sight of man but in the sight of God. The grass always looks greener on the other side, but grass is grass! You may think that running away to escape from life is a solution, but wherever you go to and whatever you do, there will be challenges. If you go by yourself, there are challenges; if God calls you to go, there will be challenges. Read and meditate on the Book of Jonah and, as you do so, ask the Lord to give you a revelation of what took place.

We have been on some journeys in the past, and may currently be on one right now, but only by the mercy of God are we able to come through:

> *Through the Lord's mercies we are not consumed, Because His compassions fail not. They are new every morning; Great is Your faithfulness. "The Lord is my portion," says my soul, "Therefore I hope in Him!"* (Lamentation 3:22-24).

There is nothing that you have done that can keep you from returning to your first love, the Lord Jesus Christ. Some journeys you take, if you do not follow Jesus, will take you past a 'small town and village mentality', where everyone knows everyone else's business! It may take you across fields where there are wolves in sheep's clothing; those who claim they are righteous and that they are the best thing since sliced bread and just what you need, but then they turn out to be something else. You will go on journeys through mazes and down all kinds of dark alleys, and you can end up in some tight spots, but return to the Lord your God!

By abiding under the shadow of the Almighty (Psalm 91), He will protect you. He will guide and lead you back onto the right path:

> *Yea, though I walk through the valley of the shadow of death, I will fear no evil; For You are with me; Your rod and Your staff, they comfort me* (Psalm 23:4).

There is nothing too hard for God.

> *"So they were offended at Him. But Jesus said to them, "A prophet is not without honor except in his own country and in his own house"* (Matthew 13:57).

You may be someone dealing with the stigma of people in your home town knowing what you used to do before you gave your life to Christ, and now you say you are a believer in Christ? Yes, now you are a believer in the Lord Jesus Christ! You do not have to say anything to anyone, just live a righteous life, and this will speak volumes. Do not let Satan hold you in condemnation, wondering what people will think or say about what you used to be - and now you are walking wholly after God? That is exactly it - what you USED TO BE! You cannot help what you were born into, but you can change *it*! When you are born again in Christ Jesus, the Bible tells us that:

> *Therefore, from now on, we regard no one according to the flesh. Even though we have known Christ according to the flesh, yet now we know Him thus no longer. Therefore, if anyone is in Christ, he is a new creation; old things have passed away; behold, all things have become new* (2 Corinthians 5:16-17).

People may have known you when you were a prodigal, recklessly, extravagant and wasteful. They will have things to say, but if you have truly moved on and you are now walking with the Lord, it should not matter to you as the word of God is all you need:

> *Yet if anyone suffers as a Christian, let him not be ashamed, but let him glorify God in this matter* (1 Peter 4:16).

You must get to the place where you can confidently say:

> *For I am persuaded that neither death nor life, nor angels nor principalities nor powers, nor things present nor things to come, nor height nor depth, nor any other created*

thing, shall be able to separate us from the love of God which is in Christ Jesus our Lord (Romans 8:38-39).

Do not worry about what others think. People will always have things to say, and if you allow that to get into your spirit, it can hold you back from reaching the level that God want you to attain in Him. One of the best things you can do when others are against you is praise and worship God! Start praising God and thanking Him for them, and you will see that whatever you are going through is minute compared to the joy you receive in Jesus Christ. Just continue to serve the Lord and live only for Him. He will not let you be ashamed, neither will He leave you nor forsake you.

If others reject you because you have decided to follow Jesus, do not worry about it - the Lord will be there for you - God's got it! This is why walking with the Lord can be a lonely walk. Not everyone will embrace you. The Holy Spirit will remove some of the people you have associated with from your life, as they may hinder God's purpose and plan for your life. They will either be removed for a season or permanently as you grow and mature in the things of God. You do not have to think about how this will be done. The Lord will orchestrate it.

He did this and still does this in my life, and I am thankful and grateful to Him. I can grow in Him at a faster rate than if I had to deal with some people at the same time! The Lord makes everything work out for the better for those who love Him. God is doing a new thing in your life:

"And have put on the new man who is renewed in knowledge according to the image of Him who created him" (Colossians 3:10).

As a believer in Christ, you may have had to leave family, loved ones or friends to follow Jesus, but it is worth it. I have had to do the same, and the Lord has never let me down yet. Through the Lord Jesus Christ, I have been able to help my family and friends come to the knowledge of Christ through His word:

> *Therefore, as the elect of God, holy and beloved, put on tender mercies, kindness, humility, meekness, longsuffering; bearing with one another, and forgiving one another, if anyone has a complaint against another;*

> *even as Christ forgave you, so you also must do* (Colossians 3:12-13).

Pray for those who despitefully use you, and love them regardless of what they may have said or done to you.

What If You Heard a Trumpet Blow From Heaven?

ARE YOU READY to meet your God? I often think that if the Lord should sound a loud trumpet now (the Shofar), would I be ready to meet Him? Am I living the life He expects of me? Pause for a moment and ask yourself these questions - think about it.

John the Baptist prepared the way for the coming of Jesus Christ. He was the link between the Old and New Testament times. What is your transforming strategy? What are you waiting for before crossing over from the things of your past into the wonderful light of the truth and eternal life? Questions, questions, questions! These questions must be asked.

As believers in Christ we must constantly check ourselves. Once you know the truth, it is this truth that will set you free. You can then, with confidence, stand on the word of God and declare:

> *For I am persuaded that neither death nor life, nor angels nor principalities nor powers, nor things present nor things to come, nor height nor depth, nor any other created thing, shall be able to separate us from the love of God which is in Christ Jesus our Lord* (Romans 8:38-39).

You must have a boldness, knowing that you want to run the race set before you and finish well. When Jesus Christ returns you should want to hear these words:

> *"His Lord said to him, 'Well done, good and faithful servant; you were faithful over a few things, I will make you ruler over many things. Enter into the joy of your Lord'* (Matthew 25:21).

What a joy! Knowing that when you hear these words you have been following the leading of the Holy Spirit, and you have fulfilled as the Bible highlights:

"And do not be conformed to this world, but be transformed by the renewing of your mind, that you may prove what is that good and acceptable and perfect will of God." (Romans 12:2)

When you are transformed through the renewing of your mind, you think differently to how the world thinks. Your language changes, your thought patterns change, you conduct yourself and interact with people differently. You also avoid places which may draw you into sinful ways. When you say "yes" to the will of God and mean it, your life will be transformed. Areas you struggled with will no longer be a struggle, as you are redeemed by the blood shed of Jesus when He died for your sins on the cross:

> *Let the redeemed of the Lord say so, Whom He has redeemed from the hand of the enemy* (Psalm 107:2).

Keep repeating this Psalm. Write it down and pin it up where you can see it as a reminder! You have been redeemed by the Lord; He says so in His word:

> *So shall My word be that goes forth from My mouth; It shall not return to Me void, but it shall accomplish what I please, and it shall prosper in the thing for which I sent it* (Isaiah 55:11).

The Lord has a 'word' over your life. Through divine revelation, you will know what it is, and as you walk in that word, you will find that you live a fulfilled life in Christ Jesus. Let Jesus take hold of your reigns. Let Him be the master of your life, and watch Him work on your behalf so that in times to come you will not have to panic when the thought comes to your mind: What if I heard a trumpet blow from heaven?

Where Is My Lot?

THE 'LOT' FELL on Zacharias to be blessed, as he administered in the Lord's temple:

> *According to the custom of the priesthood, his lot fell to burn incense when he went into the temple of the Lord* (Luke 1:9).

The lot fell on Jonah to warn the people of Nineveh:

> *Now the word of the Lord came to Jonah the son of Amittai, saying, "Arise, go to Nineveh, that great city, and cry out against it; for their wickedness has come up before Me"* (Jonah 1:1-2).

When the lot falls on you it will cause others to fear and worship God. You need to examine what your lot is in life. What has God called you to do? Discovering my purpose in life has taken me many years. The Lord will and does speak to His people about exactly what He wants them to do, which is your divine destiny. Your lot is your calling. If you have a burning passion in a particular area of work, for example, this will give you an indication of what the Lord has called you to do. Sometimes you will feel strongly against something which you see happening which is not as God would approve, again, it maybe the Lord showing you that you are the one called to do something about it.

When you yield totally to God, your life is no longer yours. This is what total surrender to God means. You give Him your life so that His will in your life can be done. Some people will only surrender some things to God, but it does not work like that. Walking fully in the things God has planned and purposed for your life takes total surrender. He does His will in your life to bring glory to Himself, He gets all the glory. It is not about us but about the Kingdom of God, winning souls for His kingdom!

When you are doing what God has called you to do, He will make provision for you to carry it out. If you make a detour like Jonah did, it will cost you and may take longer - but repenting and asking for God's forgiveness will put you back on track with Him. Ask God to lead and direct you into what He has called you to do to ensure that you are fulfilling His purpose and plan for your life.

Me, Myself and I Cannot Get Enough

THE WORLD'S WAYS and its systems are selfish. It is about 'me, myself and I'. God's kingdom is totally different; it is about others. When you are chosen by God, you immediately go into the 'Ministry of Helps'. You are called by God to reach out to others, to help and assist them in either prayer, giving your time, or resources, including money, clothing or shelter.

In these last days, the world is moving at a rapid pace. Look at retailers, for example. There is an ongoing move away from paying cash for purchases, to having a system where you have to use a card and enter your details upfront before you can purchase anything or shop on the internet. Some food retailers now package food in similar packaging which can be misleading to the customer. For example, a full fat item and a reduced fat item will sometimes be labelled and packaged in a similar way and the customer who will often have little time to check all items purchased, as we are living in a 'microwave' society will not see this subtle change. It is only when they arrive home or open the product that they notice that they have purchased the wrong item - but by this time of course, it maybe too late to return it as it has been opened!

As a believer in Christ you too have to watch out for the strategies of Satan, when he is trying to bring deception and confusion. He is a counterfeit, an imitator, a deceiver and a liar, read John 8:44. Get to know the world's way of working so that you can apply the word of God when situations arise. It is by knowing the word of God that you are 'more than a conqueror' and will have the victory.

Restriction is also used by the world to control people's lives. I once visited a garden centre with an elderly neighbour who purchased some plants and was about to pay by cheque, but the cashier told her that they no longer accept cheques, only cards or cash. Having a card at her age would mean having to memorise a four-digit personal identification number, as writing it down could put her in danger of being targeted for robbery, as would carrying a large amount of cash. There is a move towards restricting society, one in which you are required to conform to a particular way of purchasing things - otherwise, you are restricted from purchasing certain goods. It limits your choices.

Does this sound familiar? Study the Book of Revelation.

Purchasing things in this way means you cannot watch your spending. You are enticed into purchasing things without limit and can easily get into debt. If you are working to build God's kingdom, revelatory knowledge will come as to how to manage your finances. Ask the Lord before you purchase large items. He will guide you.

Joshua, Moses My Servant Is Dead!

Do you sometimes hold on to things that have passed? You have been that way before and should not attempt to go back there. Rather than renewing your mind and moving on, you seem to dwell on things that have passed, which holds you in bondage. It is good to move on from things from the past, such as hurt, mistreatment by others, selfishness, loneliness, defeat and anger, to name but a few. Do you think at times that holding on to things from the past will assist you with the future?

> *Brethren, I do not count myself to have apprehended; but one thing I do, forgetting those things which are behind and reaching forward to those things which are ahead* (Philippians 3:13).

Move on in life. Do not let the 'old' keep you in bondage, a slave to sin. You could say you are a new creation in Christ, but the renewing of your mind must be daily, just as abstaining from sin, repenting and following God's word.

Some people say they have moved on, but when they open their mouths, you really have to ask yourself, is this one of the Lord's anointed? Believers in Christ are called to be set apart, to be different. Even if you are around those who say they are believers but who are not living according to the word of God - because they are backbiting, living a dishonest life, or doing things which do not line up to the word of God – just you hold fast to the word of God. It is by your example that others become convicted, and if they truly love the Lord, they will be convicted. As a believer in Christ, do not allow yourself to become contaminated by those around you who do not live according to the word of God. This is why you must stay in the word of God, so you can know what is acceptable of God and live by it.

Another thing that may keep you from moving on in life is seeking affirmation from man. Be careful who you hook up with or enter into a covenant relationship with. If doing the things of

God means walking alone, then walk alone! Associate with those who are sold-out for God, those who know His word and are 'doers' of the word of God! That is the bottom line.

If there are people in your life who are not in tune with God, ask God to remove them from your life and to send you those who are like Him. God will send the right people into your life, so wait on the Lord. Let Philippians 3:13 be a constant reminder to you. God will hold some people behind so that you can move ahead because His will for your life must be done on earth as it is in heaven. Sometimes it may seem that you are hooked up to the devil in hell! They look saintly, they dress saintly, they smile saintly, but then they say or do something which allows you to see just who they really are. Before you go into a relationship with anyone, pray about it and ask God for discernment and wisdom.

Stay focussed and do not be contaminated by the world's standards because the world has nothing to offer but distress. Anything that can be seen is subject to change, but only the things of God which are unseen are eternal. Therefore, set your eyes on these things:

> *While we do not look at the things which are seen, but at the things which are not seen. For the things which are seen are temporary, but the things which are not seen are eternal* (2 Corinthians 4:18).

Do not lament over things which have been pruned or cut out of your life by God. To be in right standing with God, He has to mould you into what He wants you to be, by any means necessary. Depend on the Lord, and He will lead and guide you to the Promise Land.

Related Scriptures:

Numbers 27:18-23
Joshua 1:1-18
Exodus 3-7
Exodus 15:1-18
Numbers 14:11-25
Numbers 27:12-23
Deuteronomy 34:1-12.

If The Cup Had Passed In Gethsemane, I Would Have Been a Goner!

THIS SHOWS ONE of the greatest characteristics of God: His selflessness and His love for every one of us.

> *For God so loved the world that He sent His only begotten Son, that whoever believes in Him should not perish but have everlasting life*
> (John 3:16).

It is a good thing God sent His Son, Jesus Christ in the flesh, because His glory would have wiped us out if He came to sort out this place Himself! Thank you, Jesus, for going through this on my behalf and thank you for showing us that obedience to Your word is key!

God knows that by sending His only Son, Jesus Christ, to die for us, this sinful world was worth it. If you know God and trust in Him, then you will know that sending His one and only Son, someone dear to Him, must mean that He was relaying a significant message to His people.

Only those who believe that Jesus Christ is the Son of God and that He was sent by God to save the world can understand. *Only through spiritual eyes will you see*. God gave something more precious to Him than anything; His only Son, Jesus Christ, to die and then rise from the dead after three days - the ultimate sacrifice.

What has Satan given? Heartache, pain and sorrow! Satan's followers cannot see this because, firstly, some will not admit that they worship him - and, secondly, they do not acknowledge that Jesus Christ is the Son of God, but deny Him because they do not know Him. Those who are not following Christ are lost and living without hope. I was once at that stage so I know.

Spread the Good News of Jesus Christ, and tell others of His loving kindness and what He has done in your life. When you do so, He will take you to a new spiritual level in Him and His plan in your life will be fulfilled.

And the Lord will make you the head and not the tail; you shall be above only and not be beneath, if indeed you heed the commandments of the Lord your God, which I command you today, and are careful to observe them
(Deuteronomy 28:13).

Find out what the promises of God are for your life, and declare it out loud. How do you do that? By reading and meditating on the word of God, and associating and fellowshipping with other believers in Christ. When God releases something to you - the manifestation of a blessing - it is because He can trust you with it. If you do not use it for its intended purpose, then He can take it away.

You are blessed to be a blessing. What God gives you is not solely for you; that is the selfish way of thinking. It is given to you to be a blessing to others and to build His kingdom. You must, therefore, thank God for sending Jesus Christ who came as flesh and died for us all so that we can have a hope and a future.

Jesus, in the Garden of Gethsemane was fulfilling the will and purpose of God, His promise to His people. The Scripture says that John the Baptist was preparing the way of the Lord (Matthew 3:1-3). The Messiah, Jesus Christ, came to earth to die for our sins, so that whoever believes in Him will not perish but have everlasting life (John 3:16). This is one of the greatest promises made to man. The righteous in Christ, shall not die but have everlasting life.

In the Garden of Gethsemane, when the hour had come for Jesus to die for mankind, He had a moment of fear, just as an ordinary man would. Jesus prayed to God saying:

> *"Father, if it is Your will, take this cup away from Me; nevertheless not My will, but Yours, be done"* (Luke 22:42).

The cup was symbolic of the sins of the people here on earth. Jesus had a moment when He did not want to fulfil what God had sent Him to do, but by honouring what God had instructed Him to do, it was well again. He walked in obedience. Had Jesus not done the will of His Father, where would we be now? Pause and think about it.

Helped By The Aged

THOSE WHO HAVE been walking with Christ for a long time, who are mature sons and daughters having grown up in the things of Christ, should help others who are 'babes in Christ'. The word of God which mature believers in Christ receive is also for assisting others who may not yet know the Lord, or who have just surrendered their lives to Him.

Mature believers in Christ have been down the road, through trials, through valleys and the wilderness during their walk with God; they have learnt valuable lessons and received revelation that the Body of Christ so desperately needs in these times. New believers in Christ and those who are about to come into the Kingdom of God need to be nurtured. Mature believers in Christ have a responsibility to assist new believers so that they too grow to become mature in the things of God, and so that they in turn can help others. It should be a continuous cycle.

New believers need to know what to expect when they surrender their lives to God. As they begin their journey of discovery in Christ Jesus, they need to be taught what to avoid and what to aim for. They need to know that the enemy (Satan) will strategically target them, and if they are not alert, he can cause them to turn away from God. They must know that the enemy is mad because they have surrendered to God, and as they are now open to the truth, the enemy will try to terminate this. They must be taught about forgiveness of sins and that the Lord does not hold those who love Him in condemnation.

Teaching on the silence of God is essential as they will need to understand that not hearing from God does not mean total abandonment by Him, but that they should continue in His ways. God will sometimes not be near to us as He wants us to discover who we really are.

There are mature believers in Christ who should assist new believers to progress from 'milk' onto 'solids', then onto 'meat' by teaching them, for example, that humility before God is key, that when God bestows favour upon their life, the flesh can creep in and pride can then raise its ugly head. They should be taught to understand that the words of their mouth and the meditation of their heart must be acceptable to God at all times, as He is their strength and their redeemer as is written in Psalm 19:14. This will help them to grow and develop in their relationship with God.

My Testimony

When I first gave my life to Christ, I recall the Holy Spirit leading me to the following Scripture, which I know assisted my growth in Christ:

> *As obedient children, not conforming yourselves to the former lusts, as in your ignorance; but as He who called you is holy, you also be holy in all your conduct, because it is written, "Be holy, for I am holy"*
> (1 Peter 1:14-16).

God expects everyone who walks according to His word to strive to be at a place where He is. Believers in Christ are heirs of God and co-heirs with Christ:

> *The Spirit Himself bears witness with our spirit that we are children of God* (Romans 8:16).

The importance of having a life of prayer and fasting must be communicated to new believers in Christ. They should be taught that having such a life breaks the bond of wickedness, destroys yokes and removes burdens. They should also be taught the importance of not conforming to the world, but that renewing their minds on a daily basis is vital in moving to a place of intimacy with God. The reasons why moving away from sin will move them closer to God cannot be over-communicated. They need to be aware of Scriptures such as:

> *Do not love the world or the things in the world. If anyone loves the world, the love of the Father is not in him* (1 John 2:15).

All of this is a gradual process, but new believers in Christ must know what is acceptable and what is unacceptable if they are to walk according to the Spirit of God. We are here to bring the Gospel of Jesus Christ to those who do not know Christ, to build the Kingdom of God, so believers in Christ need to be equipped.

You must decrease so that God can increase. People of the world should look at a believer in Christ and acknowledge that they are indeed a child of the Most High God.

Further reading: Titus 2.

The Body of Christ - Where Are The Hands?

A BELIEVER IN Christ must extend a hand to others: to the needy, the destitute, the lonely, the depressed, the lost. Where are the hands? Hands are symbolic of authority. There are many actions that the hands do: they can wave, beckon, push, hold, catch, squeeze, clasp, feel and clap, to name a few. As part of the Body of Christ - there is a need to assist - just as the parts of our natural body operate. If you see someone in need of help, reach out and be a living example of what the Bible says. The Good Samaritan did just that:

> *But a certain Samaritan, as he journeyed, came where he was. And when he saw him, he had compassion* (Luke 10:33).

Be a samaritan for God. No matter what your calling is, you must extend a hand. Some are only concerned with doing the bare minimum. The thoughts which some entertain range from "It is my turn to do this piece of work at this time. I will only do it when it is my turn" to "I do the church's administration, so I cannot pick up a piece of paper from the floor in the sanctuary because that is for the hygiene department." Where are the hands! Some do not see outside of their remit, but the Lord would say "extend and enlarge your territory".

Jabez prayed for this to God in 1 Chronicles 4:9-10. If an unknown person such as Jabez can pray such a powerful prayer, why not those in the Body of Christ? Your pastor may call you to assist with giving a special offering for a certain project which the ministry is undertaking. Some would turn a blind eye because, as far as they are concerned, they give enough already. Extend a hand! You open yourself up to divine blessings and uncommon favour when you do over and above what is expected of you - and as you do it from your heart. Have the heart of a giver.

Remember, God is the one who enables you to get wealth, not man. (Study Deuteronomy 8). You are equipped and ready for service. This means that whatever you are called of God to do, you should do it diligently:

> *Whatever your hand finds to do, do it with your might; for there is no work or device or knowledge or wisdom in the grave where you are going* (Ecclesiastes 9:10).

Extend your hands here on earth so that your reward will be great in heaven! Someone needs you to talk to them, to help them with their shopping, to help them with their children, to help with their reading, to help bring joy back into their heart, to share a Scripture with them, to listen to the problems they are facing, to assist them in growing more in Christ, to go to church with them, to pray with them, to listen to them, to buy them something to eat, to give them a ride in your car to work or church, to help them with their budgeting, to cook some food for them, to smile with them, to cry with them, to find a good church for them, to hold their hand ... let us extend a hand!

Has Anyone Seen My Talent?

YOU HAVE BEEN chosen by God:

> *"Before I formed you in the womb I knew you; before you were born I sanctified you; I ordained you a prophet to the nations"* (Jeremiah 1:5).

God has a plan for your life! Do not just take on the things you want to do, but discover what God created you to be. What is your talent? What is your passion? Can you smile with others even when they are being horrible to you? Can you love those who despitefully use you? Can you speak to the hearts of men and make them want to change the way they feel about themselves and turn to the things of God? Discover your talent!

If you do not discover your talent for yourself, someone will give one to you; this is called labelling.

When you seek the things of God, He will give you all you need. You should use whatever God has already planted inside you to bring the lost souls to Christ:

> *There are diversities of gifts, but the same Spirit. There are differences of ministries, but the same Lord. And there are diversities of activities, but it is the same God who works all in all* (1 Corinthians 12:4-6).

No matter what you are gifted to do, it comes right back to God. It is God who gave you the talent in the first place, so you should use it for His glory alone. If you use your talent to operate in a way that is not of God, for example what seems like prophesying into your life by someone reading your palm, it is called 'divinity' or 'spirituality'. Beware of people who say that they can tell you your future by reading your palm, stay away from them - they are false prophets:

> *Beware of false prophets, who come to you in sheep's clothing, but inwardly they are ravenous wolves* (Matthew 7:15).

How can you tell the difference between false prophets and prophets of God? By their fruits:

> *You will know them by their fruits. Do men gather grapes from thorn bushes or figs from thistles? Even so, every good tree bears good fruit, but a bad tree bears bad fruit* (Matthew 7:16-17).

What type of fruits are being produced? If they bear bad fruits - things that bring fear, distress, sorrow, temporary pleasure, uncertainty or anything that is false - then they are not of God. Prophets of God bear good fruits, things that line up with the word of God and draw you closer to Him. Hold on to the word of God because:

> *The blessing of the Lord makes one rich, and He adds no sorrow with it* (Proverbs 10:22).

The word of God is truth. In everything, ask yourself, "What does the word of God say about this?" You see, a genuine believer in Christ will always give all the glory to God:

> *Not unto us, O Lord, not unto us, But to Your name give glory, because of Your mercy, because of Your truth* (Psalm 115:1).

True prophets of God are selfless. They have a love for God, a love for people and a desire to please God alone. They receive revelation from God and bring His divine word to the lost, the hurting, the lonely, the babes in Christ, those who have been walking with God for a long time, those who have a hunger for Him, those who have turned away from Him and the spiritually blind.

> *Surely the Lord does nothing, unless He reveals His secret to His servants the prophets* (Amos 3:7).

So, with this confidence, a person who obeys the word of God will humble themselves before Him.

A true believer in Christ has authority from God and is secure in who the Lord made them to be. They do not run after 'positions' in their secular jobs or in the church; it is the Lord who promotes them:

> *For evildoers shall be cut off; but those who wait on the Lord, they shall inherit the earth* (Psalm 37:9).

Therefore, whatever talent the Lord has placed within you, use it. The Lord gave this to you for a reason, to further His kingdom. It is not for you to sit back and do nothing with it. The Parable of the Talents in Matthew 25:14-30 is one to study. Some people may desire to have a job in a specific field, but because it does not come as quickly as they think it should, they do nothing and will not turn their hand to anything else whilst there are waiting. Use what you have been given from the Lord whilst you are waiting for your turn to come. Do something, and do not just bury your talent:

> *He who has a slack hand becomes poor,*
> *But the hand of the diligent makes rich*
> *(Proverbs 10:4).*

It's Not What You Do, It's What's In Your Heart

AT TIMES, A believer in Christ can feel that when they do something, they ought to get something in return; they think to themselves that the Pastor or Bishop will see it and reward me, me, me! It is God who sees your heart. It's not what you do, it's what's in your heart that matters. Walking with God is a heart matter. God is not moved by those who try to score points. God made us, and He knows what we are capable of. He gave us the Holy Bible as a guide so that we can know how to live and how to behave in order to inherit the Kingdom of God:

> *Blessed are the poor in spirit, For theirs is the kingdom of heaven* (Matthew 5:3).

This goes beyond emotions. Your spiritual well-being is key. You cannot come to God just anyhow or with any thoughts like: "Oh, it is my turn to do this piece of work, so I will just get in there, do my bit and get out." The Lord is not pleased with this type of behaviour. You must have a heart after God and follow wholly after Him. Be an imitator of what He says and does in His word to you; this is why you need to be in the word constantly to get a revelation of what it saying.

David had a heart after God (Acts 13:22). When your heart is right, you will receive from God. If you work for God knowing that you are doing it for His glory and His glory alone, He will provide all that you need to do whatever He has called you to do. If you get naturally tired, He will provide you with supernatural strength. If you do not get a chance to eat, He will keep you. This is the God I serve:

> *"If you ask anything in My name, I will do it. If you love Me, keep My commandments* (John 14:14-15).

What a great promise this is for those living for Christ! God does not lie, neither does His word return to Him void. If He said it, He will do it! When you grasp the principles of God, you can walk in abundance, which means that you will lack nothing spiritually, financially or emotionally; all of your needs will be met. You will be healthier, happier and wealthier. You will grow and mature in the things of God because you do the things of God unto God and not for man:

> *I planted, Apollos watered, but God gave the increase. So then neither he who plants is anything, nor he who waters, but God who gives the increase* (1 Corinthians 3:6-7).

Some people will turn away from God because they are men pleasers, but if you have accepted the Lord Jesus Christ as Lord and Master of your life, then He should be just that.

The problem at times can be that some are working for man rather than God, and then when it does not work out, they start blaming God! In everything you do, ask yourself, "Did I do it as unto the Lord?" If the answer is yes, then it shall be well with your soul. Before you commence anything, take it to the Lord in prayer. If you already know it is directly from God, no need to pray - just do it!

Ask God what His will for your life is, and He will direct you. You can work from dusk until dawn, but if God is not in it, forget it! You must discover what you are called to do so that you do not toil in vain:

> *Unless the Lord builds the house, They labour in vain who build it; unless the Lord guards the city, the watchman stays awake in vain* (Psalm 127:1).

Walk according to the Spirit of God.

> *Now the Lord is the Spirit; and where the Spirit of the Lord is, there is liberty*
> (2 Corinthians 3:17).

Be in the place that God called you to and not where you think you should be - you are heading for trouble if you make your own decisions just like Jonah did.

> *"There are many plans in a man's heart, nevertheless the Lord's counsel - that will stand."*
> (Proverbs 19:21)

When you are walking with the Lord, it is His word that 'goes', not yours. Let His will be done in your life - and every so often you need to repeat out loud - "Not my will Lord, but Your will be done here on earth as it is in heaven." The Bible says:

> *For I know the thoughts that I think toward you, says the Lord, thoughts of peace and not of evil, to give you a future and a hope* (Jeremiah 29:11).

This should serve as a reminder of God's intentions for you. It is not about what you want, but about what God requires of you. Ask God to reveal to you His divine purpose for your life:

> *The steps of a good man are ordered by the Lord, And He delights in his way*
> (Psalm 37:23).

God will lay upon your heart His will and purpose for your life. I once heard someone say that "An intention is not something we purpose to do, but it is something we connect to." Connect with people who are going somewhere in the Lord. If you do not know what you are called to do, you can end up burning yourself out! You can become frustrated as your heart becomes burdened, because you did not patiently wait for the Lord to instruct you. You then do the things that others say you should be doing, or you do things based on your own wisdom.

I would never have thought I could write a book, but the Lord laid this upon my heart. I know there are people who need to hear what the Spirit of God is saying at this time, and He has used me as a vessel to convey it.

I am not doing this of my own accord, it is the Holy Spirit who led me to write this book.

Reposition yourself and have a heart to humbly go before God and ask Him to direct your every step. What has God laid on your heart to do? Remember, discernment is key. If what you are doing gives all the glory to God, then it is from God; if it glorifies the flesh or man then, it is not from God. As Psalm 37:23 tells us, it is God who orders the steps of a good man. Do not rush into things thinking that it must be done now. It took me years to write this book and to publish it because preparation and timing is key.

What the Lord has placed in your heart will not make you weary:

But those who wait on the Lord shall renew their strength; They shall mount up with wings like eagles, They shall run and not be weary, They shall walk and not faint
(Isaiah 40:31).

It's not what you do, it's what's in your heart.

Are You Heading For Potiphar's House?

THE ISHMAELITES SOLD Joseph to an Egyptian by the name of Potiphar when Joseph was taken to Egypt as a slave (Genesis 39). Potiphar was a wealthy man and a high officer of Pharaoh. In time, he put Joseph in charge of his entire household. Potiphar's wife became attracted to Joseph and tried to seduce him, but Joseph rejected her advances. Because of this rejection, she falsely accused Joseph and had him imprisoned
(Genesis 39: 6-19).

Are you heading for Potiphar's house? You may have already started the journey. It may be that you said something that others became jealous of, and so they started to despise you. Like Joseph, do still love those who despitefully use you. Do not become bitter, because as the love of God grows within you for them, you will find it easy to forgive, and you will continue to progress in the things of God.

The Lord says that vengeance is His (Romans 12:19), so you do not have to fight any battles on your own or deal with those who reject you but take whatever is troubling you to the Lord in prayer. Ask the Lord to tell you when to share your plans, and with whom. Joseph's brothers plotted to kill him because he told them his dream. Like Joseph, you may be thrown into a pit by others as God unfolds your destiny and His plans for your life; others may despise you for this. You may not understand why those who should love you and rejoice with you, whom you love - start to hate you. As you are shut away, you may feel that life seems to be fading, but if you just hold on and never forget the God you serve - it shall be well!

Sometimes, God will allow things to happen to you as a test to see where you are in Him, and also for you to see what is really in your heart! It is a time of training for you. God will bring you to that place of trust in Him. If you trust and love God, you will know that no matter how long it takes, He will see you through. Just keep praising and worshipping Him and maintain a good heart.

When you seem to be shut away with those who have done all manner of things and who work according to the kingdom of darkness, you must remain in the place of praise to the Most High God. You may feel that those who you were shut away with seem to have escaped doom, and you may find yourself wondering when God is going to come through for you. It is what you do and say at this time that is going to be crucial. Do not curse God but keep on praising Him.

You may ask yourself: "How long will I be in this wilderness?" Hold on, God will see you through! You may mention to someone one day "remember me", but then months and years go by and still you are in that place of being shut away. Then finally, one day, you are called and released! Praise be to God! Because you held on and continued to praise God, you will come out of the wilderness to a place of great height. You will be promoted to great things and be made ruler over 'much' because you remained faithful with the 'little' God had entrusted you with.

During all your wilderness days, you never stopped praising God, you never stopped rejoicing for what He has done for you, you never stopped tithing or giving an offering, you never stopped helping others, you never stopped having hope - you held on to Godly wisdom which surpasses all understanding - you are on your way to Potiphar's house. Then, when the very people who despised you come begging at your door, what do you do? The word, hold on to the word of God! Welcome them and love them, because the Bible says

> "*Repay no one evil for evil. Have regard for good things in the sight of all men*" (Romans 12:17).

As a child of the Most High God, you have the victory. The battle is won! Remain in that place of humility, always before God, and He will strengthen you. No matter what others have done to you, stay in a place of love and walk in forgiveness, and you will have the victory. Check yourself. Where are you today? Are you bitter? Are you resentful? Are you walking in unforgiveness? Are you angry at the smallest of things? Where are you heading? Are you staying in a pit or are you heading for Potiphar's house?

I Used To Go To Church, But Something Happened!

ALL IS GOING well for you. You hear the word of God and you praise Him. You thank Him for opening doors of opportunity for you. You are at church at every possible opportunity, giving thanks and praising Him, walking holy and in line with what God requires of you. You tell others how good the Lord has been to you, how good He continues to be to you, and you delight in His goodness towards you. One day the word of the Lord comes forth to say that it is the "Year of Restoration and Release". The preacher explains that there will be a fight with the enemy to get all that he has stolen restored to you, and also for your release. You then become lazy because God is no longer doing what you need Him to do. You stop praising Him and instead begin to ask Him why, why, why? "Why is it that I have to fight for what belongs to me, Lord?"

Satan never stops trying - his ultimate aim is to steal, kill and destroy; this is his full-time job! God is always consistent. He is the same yesterday, today and forever - He never changes! Man, however, does change. Man always wants more, more, more. If you are single, you may ask God why you do not yet have a partner, and you may even become angry with God. If you are married and your husband or wife is not saved, that is, have not surrendered their life to Christ, you may ask God why he or she is not coming to church and giving their life to God?

God will release things to you when you are able to handle it! Everything has a price and you must pay to have it, no matter what it is - that is just how it is. If you get something too quickly, or for free, you may not appreciate its value or know how to handle it - because you did not pay for it or receive a revelation about it.

Think about what Jesus did for us on the cross. He paid a huge price just for you and for me. Walking wholly with the Lord Jesus means that there is a price to pay. It means that you cannot do the things you did when you were of the world. When God gives revelation to His people through His prophets or through His word in the Bible, they can sometimes find it too much and give up. They find communing with Him or even going to church too much! If you truly believe and trust in God, you will rely on Him completely.

When you begin to give up, you then start to pull away from church. Attending church now seems like a chore, as you feel that God is not hearing you and not releasing to you the things you think you deserve. This is when doubt starts to kick in; however, the Bible tells us:

> *But without faith it is impossible to please Him, for he who comes to God must believe that He is, and that He is a rewarder of those who diligently seek Him.* (Hebrews 11:6)

At times, you may even blame the devil for what you are going through, not realising that it is God who is dealing with you!

Have your prayers been in vain? No. The Lord knows your heart. He knows what you are about, and He knows when you are worshipping Him just for what you can get from Him. The word of God has the power to penetrate right through you, and if you are pretending, the thoughts and intents of the heart will be revealed. You may end up feeling convicted, yet rather than dealing with it and asking God for forgiveness so you can move back into alignment with His will, you start to pull away from church, from fellowshipping with God and others.

I met a woman once through a divine appointment, and during our conversation the subject of attending church came up. She tells me she no longer goes to church. She said, "I used to attend church but something happened." But she either could not or did not want to explain exactly what happened to cause her to stop attending church. This shows that discernment is key when you are walking with the Lord, otherwise the enemy will come in and steal all that you have learnt from the word of God. The Bible talks about the type of ground that the word of God is sown into. Read and study this in Matthew 13:3-9, the parable of the sower.

When the word of God is heard or read, it will have an effect on you. The word of God when it is heard by those who are in a 'stony place' - meaning a place where there is not much soil - will immediately spring up pre-maturely. But then when the heat is turned up the word is burnt out of them. They then lose focus and blame others or blame God, and soon stop coming to church. They stop reading the Bible and calling on the name of Jesus and instead begin to blame God.

To keep your spiritual sword sharp, remain in the word and be doers of the word! The Bible says that the word of God brings light. If you hear the word of God and there is still darkness, then you need to check yourself because the word of God never lies - it is truth. When you are going through trials or testing, this is when you need to go to church the most. Do not draw back as it is the strategy of the enemy to abort the things of God that have been imparted to you.

If you do not know Jesus Christ and what you have read in this book is pulling at your heart strings, then pray to God right now. Ask Him to help you with whatever you are struggling with and ask Him to come into your life right now if you do not yet know Him, He is waiting for you:

Dear Lord Jesus,

Thank you for bringing Your word to me at a time when I needed it. I believe that Jesus Christ is the Son of God and that He died for my sins. I ask you to help me with *[name your struggle(s) here].* I repent of my sins, and I submit my life to You and ask for Your forgiveness. Come into my heart today, be God of my life and make me clean and whole.

In Jesus' name.

Amen.

For more titles from Avril Hall please see

www.avrilhallglobal.com

Published by Avril Hall
Printed in Great Britain

Do write to me at ***info@avrilhallglobal.com*** *and let me know your thoughts on what I have written through the divinely inspired leading of the Holy Spirit, and remember: Only through spiritual eyes will you see - messages.*
God bless you.

Notes:

Notes:

Notes:

Notes:

Notes:

Notes:

Notes:

Notes:

Notes:

Notes:

Notes:

Notes:

Notes:

Notes:

Notes:

Notes:

Notes:

Notes:

Notes:

Notes:

Notes:

Notes:

www.ingramcontent.com/pod-product-compliance
Ingram Content Group UK Ltd.
Pitfield, Milton Keynes, MK11 3LW, UK
UKHW041825200726
13854UKWH00002BA/560

9 780955 994432